Tus cinco sentidos y tu sexto sentido | **Your Five Senses and Your Sixth Sense**

El olfato

Smell

Clara Reade

Traducción al español: Eida de la Vega

PowerKiDS press.

New York

Published in 2014 by The Rosen Publishing Group, Inc.
29 East 21st Street, New York, NY 10010

First Edition

Editor: Jennifer Way and Amelie von Zumbusch
Book Design: Kate Vlachos
Photo Research: Katie Stryker

Traducción al español: Eida de la Vega

Photo Credits: Cover Paul Bradbury/OJO Images/Getty Images; p. 4 Yellow Dog Productions/Lifesize/Getty Images; p. 7 Monkey Business Images/Shutterstock.com; pp. 8, 24 (nose) DigitalFabiani/Shutterstock.com; p. 11 zhuda/Shutterstock.com; p. 12 Dmitry Kalinovsky/Shutterstock.com; pp. 15, 24 (smoke) Michael Blann/Digital Vision/Getty Images; p. 16 Zurijeta/Shutterstock.com; p. 19 ying/Shutterstock.com; p. 20 Dennis Donohue/Shutterstock.com; pp. 23, 24 (tongue) Purestock/Thinkstock.

Library of Congress Cataloging-in-Publication Data

Reade, Clara, author.
  Smell = El olfato / by Clara Reade ; translated by Eida de la Vega. — First edition.
     pages cm. — (Your five senses and your sixth sense = Tus cinco sentidos y tu sexto sentido)
English and Spanish.
Includes index.
ISBN 978-1-4777-3277-9 (library)
1. Odors—Juvenile literature. 2. Smell—Juvenile literature. 3. Animal defenses—Juvenile literature. I. Vega, Eida de la, translator. II. Reade, Clara. Smell. III. Reade, Clara. Smell. Spanish. IV. Title. V. Title: Olfato.
QP458.R4318 2014
612.8'6–dc23
                              2013022461

Websites: Due to the changing nature of Internet links, PowerKids Press has developed an online list of websites related to the subject of this book. This site is updated regularly. Please use this link to access the list: www.powerkidslinks.com/yfsyss/smell/

Manufactured in the United States of America

CPSIA Compliance Information: Batch #W14PK3: For Further Information contact Rosen Publishing, New York, New York at 1-800-237-9932

Tus cinco sentidos y tu sexto sentido | Your Five Senses and Your Sixth Sense

El olfato

Smell

Clara Reade

Traducción al español: Eida de la Vega

PowerKiDS
press™

New York

Published in 2014 by The Rosen Publishing Group, Inc.
29 East 21st Street, New York, NY 10010

First Edition

Editor: Jennifer Way and Amelie von Zumbusch
Book Design: Kate Vlachos
Photo Research: Katie Stryker

Traducción al español: Eida de la Vega

Photo Credits: Cover Paul Bradbury/OJO Images/Getty Images; p. 4 Yellow Dog Productions/Lifesize/Getty Images; p. 7 Monkey Business Images/Shutterstock.com; pp. 8, 24 (nose) DigitalFabiani/Shutterstock.com; p. 11 zhuda/Shutterstock.com; p. 12 Dmitry Kalinovsky/Shutterstock.com; pp. 15, 24 (smoke) Michael Blann/Digital Vision/Getty Images; p. 16 Zurijeta/Shutterstock.com; p. 19 ying/Shutterstock.com; p. 20 Dennis Donohue/Shutterstock.com; pp. 23, 24 (tongue) Purestock/Thinkstock.

Library of Congress Cataloging-in-Publication Data

Reade, Clara, author.
 Smell = El olfato / by Clara Reade ; translated by Eida de la Vega. — First edition.
    pages cm. — (Your five senses and your sixth sense = Tus cinco sentidos y tu sexto sentido)
 English and Spanish.
 Includes index.
 ISBN 978-1-4777-3277-9 (library)
 1. Odors—Juvenile literature. 2. Smell—Juvenile literature. 3. Animal defenses—Juvenile literature. I. Vega, Eida de la, translator. II. Reade, Clara. Smell. III. Reade, Clara. Smell. Spanish. IV. Title. V. Title: Olfato.
 QP458.R4318 2014
 612.8'6—dc23
                                    2013022461

Websites: Due to the changing nature of Internet links, PowerKids Press has developed an online list of websites related to the subject of this book. This site is updated regularly. Please use this link to access the list: www.powerkidslinks.com/yfsyss/smell/

Manufactured in the United States of America

CPSIA Compliance Information: Batch #W14PK3: For Further Information contact Rosen Publishing, New York, New York at 1-800-237-9932

CONTENIDO

CONTENTS

4

El olfato es uno de tus cinco sentidos.
Los otros son el gusto, el tacto, la vista y el oído.

Smell is one of the five senses.
The others are taste, touch, sight, and hearing.

5

Hueles con la **nariz**. El olfato también usa el cerebro.

You smell with your **nose**. Smelling uses your brain, too.

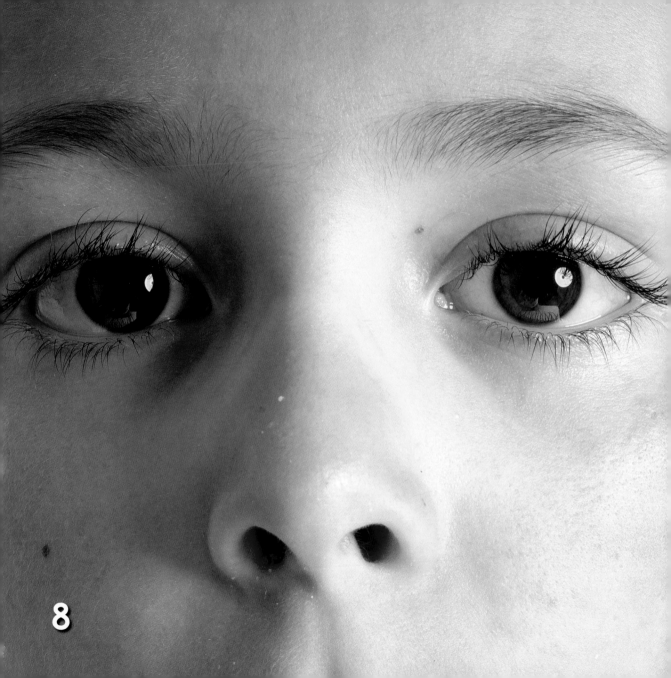

8

La baba que tienes en la nariz se llama moco. Ayuda a tu nariz a captar los olores.

The slime in your nose is called mucus. It helps your nose pick up smells.

Las personas que no pueden sentir los olores tienen anosmia.

People who cannot smell have anosmia.

11

La mayoría de las personas puede distinguir alrededor de 10,000 olores diferentes.

Most people can smell about 10,000 different smells.

13

Algunos olores nos alertan del peligro.
Si olemos **humo**, es posible que haya un fuego.

Some smells warn you of danger. If you smell **smoke**, there may be a fire.

15

Cuando tienes catarro es difícil distinguir los olores.

When you have a cold, it is harder to smell things.

17

El gusto y el olfato están ligados. Por eso no puedes distinguir bien los sabores cuando tienes catarro.

Taste and smell are linked. That is why you cannot taste well when you have a cold.

19

Los osos son los animales terrestres con el mejor olfato.

Bears have the best sense of smell of any land animal.

Las serpientes huelen
con la **lengua**.

Snakes smell with their **tongues**.

23

PALABRAS QUE DEBES SABER / WORDS TO KNOW

(la) nariz
nose

(el) humo
smoke

(la) lengua
tongue